W9-BMU-708

Table of Contents

Plumbers at Work

Reed wants to be a plumber.

What do they do?

They put in pipes.

They fix leaks.

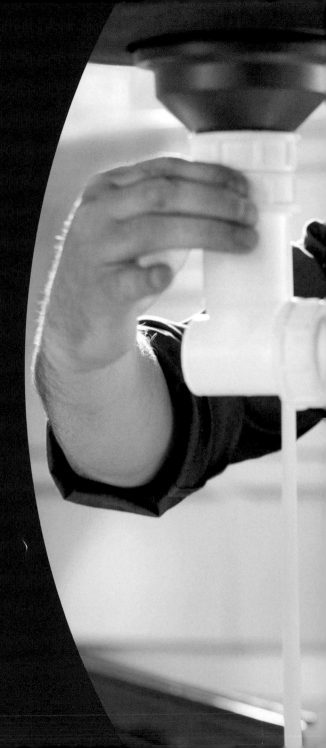

pipe

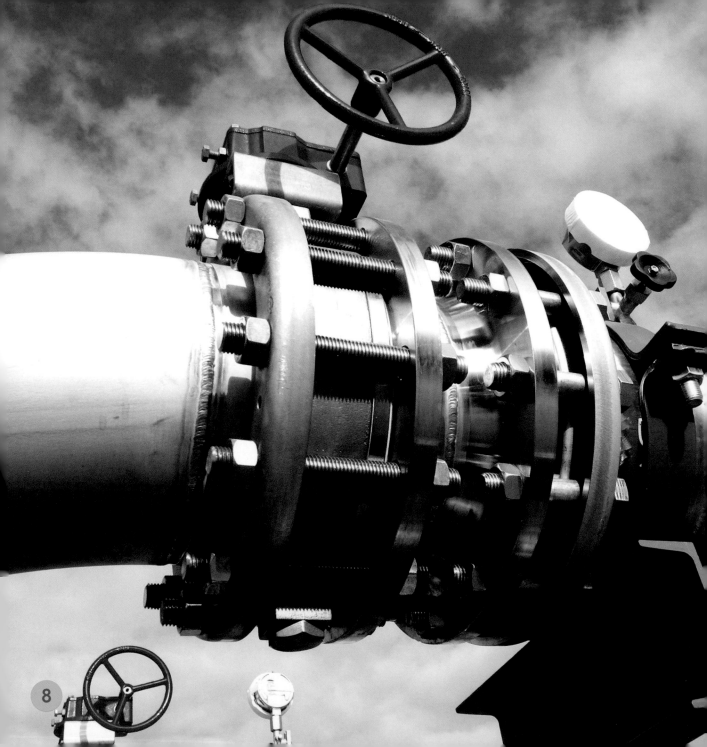

Pipes bring water
into buildings.

Pipes take water
out too.

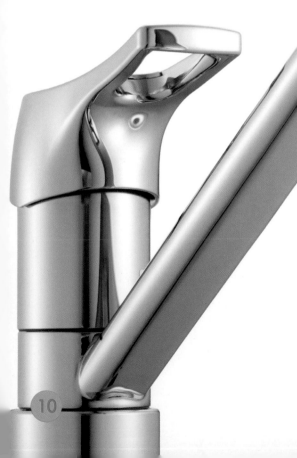

Drip! Drip!
A sink leaks.
Max can fix it.

He puts in a new part.
Done!

water heater

Brr. The shower is cold.

There is no hot water.

Gus can fix it.

He puts in a new water heater.

The city wants a new rec center.

May makes a plan.

She knows where to put the pipes.

plan

There is a new hospital.
Pat puts in sprinklers.

sprinkler

If there is a fire,
water will spray.

Oh, no! A pipe broke!

Water is everywhere.

Vic can fix it.

He puts in a new pipe.

Plumbers do good work.

In a Plumber's Tool Kit

work bench
Plumbers use a work bench to fix and clean pipes before putting them in.

tool belt
Plumbers use a belt to keep tools handy.

pipe wrench
A pipe wrench can grab pipes of different sizes.

pipes
Plumbers carry small parts of pipes to make quick repairs.

Picture Glossary

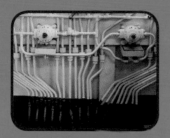

pipes
Long, hollow tubes used to carry water.

sprinkler
A faucet in the walls and ceilings that will spray water if there is a fire in a building.

rec center
A place with a gym, a pool, and other areas for activities and games.

water heater
A water tank that heats up water; it sends hot water out of the faucet.

Index

To Learn More

Learning more is as easy as 1, 2, 3.

1) Go to www.factsurfer.com

2) Enter "plumbers" into the search box.

3) Click the "Surf" button to see a list of websites.

With factsurfer.com, finding more information is just a click away.

Ideas for Parents and Teachers

Bullfrog Books let children practice reading informational text at the earliest reading levels. Repetition, familiar words, and photo labels support early readers.

Before Reading
- Discuss the cover photo. What does it tell them?
- Look at the picture glossary together. Read and discuss the words.

Read the Book
- "Walk" through the book and look at the photos. Let the child ask questions. Point out the photo labels.
- Read the book to the child, or have him or her read independently.

After Reading
- Prompt the child to think more. Ask: Do you know anyone who is a plumber? What other kinds of jobs might a plumber do?

Bullfrog Books are published by Jump!
5357 Penn Avenue South
Minneapolis, MN 55419
www.jumplibrary.com

Library of Congress Cataloging-in-Publication Data
Meister, Cari, author.
  Plumbers / by Cari Meister.
    pages cm.—(Community helpers)
  Summary: "This photo-illustrated book for early readers describes what plumbers do to install and maintain water systems in homes and in the community"—Provided by publisher.
  Audience: Ages 5-8.
  Audience: K to grade 3.
  Includes bibliographical references and index.
  ISBN 978-1-62031-095-3 (hardcover)
  ISBN 978-1-62496-150-2 (ebook)
  ISBN 978-1-62031-139-4 (paperback)
  1. Plumbers—Juvenile literature.
  2. Plumbing—Juvenile literature. I. Title.
  HD8039.P62M45 2015
  696.1092—dc23

                          2013044262

Editor: Wendy Dieker
Series Designer: Ellen Huber
Book Designer: Lindaanne Donohoe
Photo Researcher: Kurtis Kinneman

Photo Credits: All photos by Shutterstock except: Corbis, 4; iStockPhoto, 1, 20t; SuperStock, 6-7, 9, 21

Printed in the United States of America at Corporate Graphics, North Mankato, Minnesota.
6-2014
10 9 8 7 6 5 4 3 2 1

Community Helpers
Plumbers

by Cari Meister

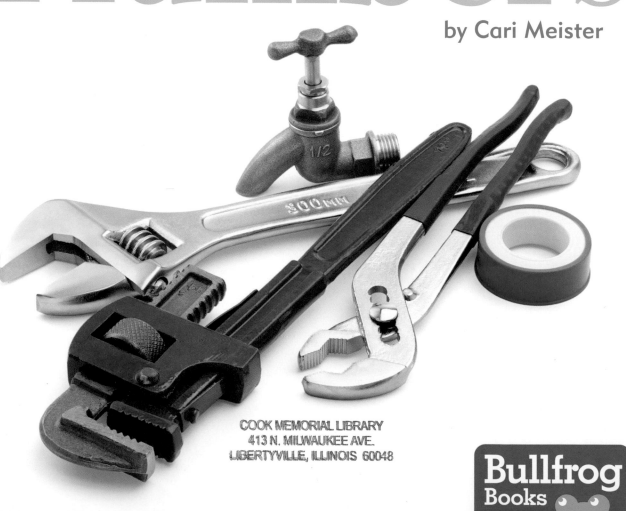

Bullfrog
Books